LYNN ROBERSON

Hearts-Ease

The Beautiful Truth

Quantum
Discovery
A LITERARY AGENCY

Hearts-Ease: The Beautiful Truth
Copyright © 2023 by Lynn Roberson

ISBN
978-1-961601-97-0 (Paperback)
978-1-961601-98-7 (eBook)

Table of Contents

The Beautiful Truth.. 1

An Honest Prayer... 2

Jesus Loves You 3

The Prayer.. 5

Receiving 7

Redemption 9

Blessed Assurance.. 10

Pets In Heaven 12

Prayer for Belonging... 14

Blessing... 15

It Is Known To The Lord... 17

Receiving Grace 19

Rest... 20

Ana 21

Being Still 23

Security... 24

The Cross.. 25

A Small Miracle 27

Angels 28

In God's Time... 29

Banjo 31

Homesick... 33

Repentance 35

Crisis Of Faith 37

Discovery 39

Belonging.. 41

One Thing I Know 42

Trust 43

Mercy.. 45

Dreams 46

Near-Death Moments 47

Where This World Ends 48

Hearts-Ease.. 50

Believing.. 52

Be Still 53

Heaven... 54

More Dreams.. 55

Other Dreams.. 57

Jane... 59

Jesus.. 60

Dreams Continued... 61

Animals And Heaven 62

Redeeming Love.. 63

Eden Redeemed A Sonnet 64

Redeeming Love A Sonnet 65

An Intercessor 67

Diamond In The Dark.. 69

The Secret Things... 71

Home... 72

Blessings For You 73

*

There is a lovely, small flower which adds color and cheer to any garden or byway. Sometimes it is called Viola. Or, whimsically, Johnny-Jump-Up. My favorite name is the old European one: Hearts-Ease.

In the folklore of flowers, the flower Hearts-Ease has many meanings—tranquility, peace of mind, restfulness. Qualities that we all yearn to possess.

In my experience, Hearts-Ease can only come when one discovers *the beautiful truth* in all its wonder. So… we will start there.

*

The Beautiful Truth

Willie Lee was an elderly lady in a local nursing home which I used to visit every Sunday. Because of diabetes, she'd had to have one leg amputated. But she never complained.

Whenever I came to visit, Willie Lee would turn off the TV in her room so we could talk about God and pray together.

One day, Willie Lee used an expression I had never heard before. She was talking about the goodness and faithfulness of God. She finished with a graceful wave of her hand and the words "Darlin', it's the *beautiful truth!*"

I loved the sound of those words!

*

Willie always spoke very slowly and graciously.

"*Our* Jesus," she would say, "He loves us *all*. And He loves us all the *time*. Sweetie—it's the *beautiful truth!*" I can still hear her as if it were yesterday—her low, patient voice speaking the words which first snagged my heart and are now engraved upon it.

Thank you, Willie Lee, for helping me to understand the *beautiful truth*.

*

An Honest Prayer

I have loved writing this little book. God gave me joy and inspiration and guided me to the scriptures He wanted to include. It has been the most wonderful experience! But it didn't start out that way.

Dear Lord….I am here. I am waiting to write your book. I should be already writing. But I have no enthusiasm. At all. Please give me a vision for this book. Please place it in my heart. I have waited too long to do your will and write it. Please help me. I don't even *want* to write it. Please, Lord, give me enough enthusiasm to at least start. Thank you.

*

By nightfall I had typed eleven pages. *Thank you* for answered prayer, Father God!

*

Jesus Loves You

How do you begin to *know* that Jesus really loves you? With a deep, delighted, forever kind of love? A special love. First, simply talk to Him. Ask Him to show you. "Ask that ye may receive, that your joy may be full." John 16:24.

Ask Him to put the absolute certainty—the *blessed assurance* of it—in your heart. He will.

St. Augustine said, "He loves each of us as if there were only one of us." And it's true.

You are as precious to God as an only child. Jesus would have died on the cross to save just you, or just me.

It's staggering, isn't it? We can't imagine such a love; and yet, in it "we move and breathe and have our being." Acts 17:28.

In my home I have pictures of Jesus the Good Shepherd, Christ gazing at the rich young ruler, and one almost life size portrait of just His face. Plus several other smaller pictures of the cross, the Holy family and—well, you get the idea.

These don't really fit into my country decor, but they are visual reminders of His presence and love. I can't imagine my home without them.

They are so meaningful to me that when my dear husband Ron and I had our baby daughter at home, I used the portrait of Christ as my focal point.

We also phoned people, asking them to please start praying.

It was a beautiful, all natural birth. I started in mild labor at 1:00 a.m. At 7:30 a.m. I called my midwife to come. The midwife said we should have a baby by nightfall—six o'clock, she estimated. We made more phone calls!

Our precious little girl, Ana, was born at 12:20 on a bright and shiny Sunday noon, just as people were getting out of their churches and chatting in the parking lots.

We had friends in. We sang worship songs. I couldn't stop looking into my baby's beautiful wide-awake eyes. She was a priceless miracle.

And we churned ice cream.

I guess I've given away the fact that I'm not a very conventional person. But I'm the way God made me. That day was one of the absolute high points of my entire life! A crucial part of it was the picture of Jesus which I used for my focal point.

But you don't need pictures. You just need a willing heart. You need to be willing to *receive* a love beyond your imagination, a love you know you could never earn. Love that He is waiting to pour over you and into you like living water to the thirsty.

*

The Prayer

In a beautifully written prayer I came across some years ago, I found something that amazed me and actually changed my life forever.

The lines of the prayer seemed simple enough at first:

Jesus, have mercy on us.

Jesus, I trust in you.

Jesus, help me love you more.

Then came the unexpected line:

Jesus, I believe in your tender love for me.

Whoa. His tender love for me! Could I pray that? It was presumptuous!(wasn't it?) I felt awkward trying to pray those words.

Of course, I believed that Jesus loved me. I had received His love the moment I gave my life to Him at a Baptist youth picnic.

But *tender* love?

For awhile I just skipped that line. But it nagged at my heart. Somehow I knew that my whole life depended on it.

I wasn't worthy of His tender love for me. I knew that. How could I possibly pray that line of the prayer?

Then the Lord, in His overflowing grace, reminded me of Mark 9:21-24, when Jesus healed the epileptic boy.

Jesus told the father, "All things are possible to him who believes."

"And straightway the father cried out, and said *with tears*, 'Lord, I believe; help thou mine *unbelief*.'"

You know his heart was broken for his child. He was desperate for help. And he was humble, not trying to deny how hard it was for him to fully believe that anything or anyone could heal the boy.

And wonderful, faithful Jesus accepted his prayer, imperfect as it was, and healed his child completely!

"Lord, I believe; help Thou mine unbelief!"

I considered that father's prayer with awe. I knew it was God who had brought it to my mind and guided me, in His great patience, to add it to my prayer—a kind of disclaimer for me to use, while He helped me to believe more fully.

So, for a time, I prayed that way:

"Jesus, I believe in your tender love for me. Help Thou mine unbelief."

I prayed this for a long, long time. He seemed to promise me that a day would come when I wouldn't need any qualification, when I would believe one hundred percent—when His love would overflow me, like the verse, "he who believes in me, out of his heart shall flow rivers of living water." John 7:38.

As always, God was true to his word. Today, with all my weaknesses and flaws, I can pray that line of the original prayer without a trace of doubt.

My heart has absorbed the *beautiful truth*.

*

I am asking you to pray this prayer out loud every day: "Jesus, I believe in your tender love for me. Help Thou mine unbelief."

Your miracle will come. You will truly know, as much as the human mind and spirit *can* know, how dearly valuable you are to Him.

Jesus says to you today: "Fear not, for I have redeemed you; I have called you by name; *you are Mine*...because you are precious in My eyes, and honored, and I love you."

Isaiah 43:1,4.

*

Receiving

In John 15:9, Jesus says these words: "As the Father has loved me, so have I loved you. Abide in my love." Jesus loves you as much as Father God loves Him! It is a lot to believe! We all need His help for faith in such an overwhelming concept.

But it *is* true. All through the Bible are promises of His steadfast love and faithfulness. We *can* abide in His love, for we have been redeemed by our Savior Jesus.

We only need to *receive* the gift.

Receiving is not always easy. It can require a kind of humility to which we are not accustomed.

I've learned so much from the elderly and from the special-needs people in my life.

Many years back I was with a church group that weekly visited a small group home for special-needs adults. The group leader presented a Bible lesson and prayer. After that I played the piano while the residents sang familiar hymns.

In the living room of the house which these few people shared, there was limited seating. One sofa, one padded rocking chair, and numerous metal folding chairs. I always took a folding chair.

One day when we arrived Annie Mae was occupying the cushioned rocking chair. As soon as she saw me, she leapt to her feet and indicated she'd been saving the chair for me.

I was chagrined. I was young at the time, and I knew these residents had aches and pains I didn't have. How brazen it would be to take the best chair!

I started to decline, I *wanted* to decline—but the Lord checked me.

"She has nothing else to give you," He spoke quietly to my spirit. "She is so proud and happy to give you this. Don't take that away from her."

So I thanked her and accepted the rocking chair. I am sure I was blushing madly, I was so humiliated. My friends all took folding chairs, and here I sat in the best chair in the house.

Receiving. It can be hard. Something makes us willing to give abundantly, while we balk at receiving.

However, to know the rest and the love of the Lord, we have to get past this false pride. We have to receive enormously and undeservedly and humbly. We are all sinners. The degree or the type of sins—well, it is an infinite number. Mostly we do the best we can, and hope God is pleased. But this is not the Way. The Way is to admit we have failed and thankfully accept Christ's rescue of us. *That* is *salvation*. That is *grace*. And there is still so much more good news!

*

Redemption

It hurts my heart to hear a Christian say, "I hope I'll get to heaven. I don't know, though, I've done a lot of wrong things in my life."

Friend, it's not about what *you* have done. It's about what *Jesus Christ* has done.

When we confess our sins and ask forgiveness, we *receive* it—our sins are gone forever! God himself does not keep them in His memory. You are not only saved, you are redeemed. You are better than you were before the mishaps happened. How? Because you have received the precious grace of Jesus, you have been bathed in His mercy. You are a new creature in Christ. 2 Cor.5:16-18. All you have to do is believe. And if you have trouble believing, He will even patiently help you with *that*.

In fact, if you have come to Him and asked forgiveness, you *belong* to Him now. You are His own child. The "fruit of the travail of His soul." Isaiah 53:11. At salvation, He takes you into His family, forever. Nothing can snatch you out of His hand. John 10:28,29. My wise friend Jane used to add, "Not even yourself." How completely reassuring!

This is the Good News of the Gospel. The beautiful truth. But there is still more!

*

Blessed Assurance

The words "*blessed assurance*" are best known from a hymn written by a blind Christian lady, Fanny J. Crosby:

"Blessed assurance, Jesus is mine! Oh, what a foretaste of glory divine! Heir of salvation, purchase of God; born of His Spirit, washed in His blood. This is my story, this is my song; praising my Savior, all the day long… perfect submission, all is at rest. I in my Savior am happy and blessed…watching and waiting, looking above, filled with His goodness, lost in His love…"

The term *blessed assurance* sounds old fashioned to some of us, because the hymn is so familiar. But what a wonderful concept. It is all of one fabric: heart-rest, trust, assurance, belonging. You can believe. Because it is the *beautiful truth*.

Let's look at what the Bible says about the redeemed of the Lord.

"Thou wilt cast all my sins into the depths of the sea." Micah 7:19

Paul reports,"But I received mercy…and the grace of the Lord overflowed for me with the faith and love that are in Christ Jesus. This saying is sure and worthy of full acceptance, that Christ Jesus came into the world to save sinners. And I am the foremost of sinners, but I received mercy…" 1 Timothy 1:13-15

We have been"delivered from the dominion of darkness and transferred to the kingdom of His beloved Son, in whom we have redemption, the forgiveness of sins." Colossians 1:13,14.

"For once you were darkness, but now you are light in the Lord. Walk as children of light." Ephesians 5:8.

So we are all in the same boat. When Adam and Eve sinned, we all fell. But God made a way, through the cross of Jesus, to bring us back into His kingdom of Light and Life!

What do you have to do? Only believe. And remember, you do not have to even do *that* all on your own. God will help you.

*

Pets In Heaven

I have had dreams about my pets and Heaven, too. We used to have a mixed breed dog that looked like a miniature English Sheepdog. His hair covered his eyes completely until we trimmed it. This dog was so loving! He grew old and died and some time much later I dreamed of him.

In the dream I had just entered Heaven and I saw my dog running excitedly toward me over rolling emerald green hills. He kept one front paw up in the air, so that it looked rather like he was dancing. This was a holdover from his years on earth, when he did the same thing if he was very excited.

That was the whole dream, nothing more. But it gave me great assurance—blessed assurance.

*

As we go through this narrative, you will find me repeating key phrases such as blessed assurance, wondrous love, rest, beautiful Truth. I realize I repeat them a lot. I want them to become second nature to you. Something which you know is real and which can be yours for the asking.

For the asking? Yes.

"Ask and ye shall receive, that your joy may be full." John 16:24.

Joy honors God. He loves for us to be happy. He especially loves it when we remember to thank Him for the blessings that have brought us joy.

The Bible talks very much about thankfulness. It is right up there with trust in its value to God.

When Jesus healed the ten lepers in Luke 17:11-19, only one returned to thank Him. He appears to be saddened by this. However, He doesn't revoke the healing of the other nine. They are blessed. But the one who returned was surely more blessed.

Colossians 3:17 tells us, "And whatever you do in word or deed, do everything in the name of the Lord Jesus, *giving thanks* to God the Father through Him."

1 Thessalonians 5:18 "Give thanks in all circumstances, for this is the will of God concerning you."

I remember on one occasion reading that last verse and taking it quite literally—feeling that God was speaking directly to me.

Give thanks when we are suffering?

Give thanks in *all* circumstances?

Yes, we can. Because we know from Romans 8:28 that God is working *everything* together for our good. That's where trust links up with thanksgiving. It is part of the beautiful truth.

I'm sure Willie Lee, the diabetic lady at the nursing home, didn't give thanks for having her leg amputated—but she gave thanks that her life was thus saved.

The Word says give thanks *in* or during all circumstances. We are not expected to be thankful *for* everything that happens, but in the presence of everything that happens.

*

Christ didn't prefer to go to the cross. We know this from his prayer in Gethsemane. But because He knew there was no other way to rescue us, He embraced his destiny. What was He thankful for? The *ability* to save you and me and all the world.

The Bible says, "He(Jesus) shall look on the fruit of the travail of His soul and be satisfied." Like a mother gazing lovingly at a newborn infant. We are the fruit of Christ's travail. And He loves us infinitely.

Would He have gone to the cross to save just one person? Just you? Just me? Yes. So great is His love.

*

Prayer for Belonging

I f you do not yet know Jesus as your Lord and Savior, and you want to, here is a prayer you can pray right now, wherever you are:

*

Jesus, I never realized how much and how tenderly you love me. I want to belong to you and to your Kingdom. Please come into my life today, forgive all my sins and heal my heart. Be my Lord, my Savior, and my dearest Friend. I thank you for hearing and answering my prayer. I receive and I believe. For it is in your Name, Jesus, that I pray. Amen.

*

If you just prayed this prayer, you are now a child of the Most High God—redeemed, washed whiter than snow.

You may or may not feel any difference immediately. But as the days go by, you will begin to know that you are a new creature in Christ.

The quickest way to really feel like His child?

Thank God every morning that you are part of His family now. Thank Him that your sins are all forgiven and forgotten. Thank Him that He will walk through this day with you, helping you in everything that you encounter.

Thankfulness is life-changing.

*

Blessing

On the subject of prayer, I learned an amazing lesson one day when I went shopping, alone, for a doll for my daughter. When I got to the register I realized I had changed purses earlier that day and had neglected to transfer my driver's license and a few other things. I tried to write a check for the doll, but the saleslady could not accept the check without my license—which I understood. What I *didn't* understand was that she not only refused, she berated me angrily for leaving home without my license or other identification. She seemed to take it as a personal affront. She was just *rude*! I'd never experienced such abrasiveness from a total stranger before.

I walked out, feeling my blood pressure rise sharply, and got into my car to drive home for my other purse. My heart was pounding. I was embarrassed and steaming hot with indignation. Whatever happened to showing courtesy to a customer, even if they weren't right? This woman had just totally chewed me out for not having my license!

Immediately these words came to my mind:"Bless and do not curse." Romans 12:14.

I wanted to say, "Not now, Lord—please not now."

But it was too late. I already knew I would have to pray a blessing on the crabby cash register lady. I gritted my teeth and mumbled in begrudging obedience, which I doubted even counted.

Then, suddenly, my heart was in tune with my Lord Jesus. He was speaking to me in my inner being. My vital signs quickly calmed down. To my wonderment, the Lord communicated to me that He had needed someone to pray for that lady, for reasons of His own, and He had no one else at that moment in time whom He could trust to do the job. He allowed her to be abrasive toward me in order to get my attention.

I began to pray everything I could think of concerning her. Blessing, salvation, healing, deliverance, comfort—whatever the Holy Spirit led me to pray.

Meanwhile the saleslady must have regretted her sharpness. When I got back with the needed I.D. she was marginally pleasant. And I gave her a smile.

Think of all the things that lady might have been facing that day. A quarrel with her teenage daughter; a husband wanting a divorce; bills she could not pay; dental work left too long undone; a migraine—the list goes on. I didn't have to know the specific need. I knew the One who knew all about it.

*

It Is Known
To The Lord

N ow, that reminds me of Claude. He was a little gnome of a fellow, an older man with streaming white hair who had once been a missionary in China. In his later years he had gotten into the same New Age group I frequented during the time when I was off the path. Like me, Claude loved Jesus but he wasn't attending church regularly, and his theology(and mine) was blurry.

On long car-pooling trips to the Light Center, Claude would patiently listen to someone's troubles and worries, smiling and nodding. I think we expected great wisdom in reply. And we got it. But not the personal and attentive answer we hoped for.

Claude would smile widely and say, "The Lord knows all about it!"

That was all.

So maybe that was his"one thing I know." His cornerstone. He was a happy, lively little man who ate cottage cheese and honey when he stopped over at our house.

Okay, if you've recovered from *that* image—it tastes just like it sounds—I want to share with you a verse I found in an obscure book of the Bible that reiterates Claude's wisdom—even more concisely.

Zechariah 14:7 says in parenthesis "it is known to the Lord."

I love that!*"It is known to the Lord!"* You bet it is. The Lord knows all about it. And He knows what to do about it, too, praise God!

I have to give you a hint what Zechariah was talking about. Because I love everything about Heaven so much. He's describing, as far as I can tell, what it will be like.

"On that day there shall be neither cold nor frost. And there shall be continuous day(it is known to the Lord), not day and not night, for at evening time there shall be light." Zechariah 14:6-7.

We won't need sunglasses anymore. During the bright times, the light will be more brilliant than we can imagine, yet it will be gentle to our eyes. During the evening(and what would be night) there is a pleasantly subdued light, this verse tells us, such as I imagine being just right for strolls and resting.

I have my imaginings—but I'm glad the Lord knows all about it.

*

Receiving Grace

Receiving grace can be hard, yes. There is something within us that resists being the recipient of something much greater than we can ever repay. It feels like charity. And the grace we receive from God is exactly that. Charity, the word used in the Old English to mean: Love.

When we become a Christian, Christ extends infinite grace to us. He washes us clean of all our past failures and all our regrets. Everything.

"Come now and let us reason together, saith the Lord. Though your sins are like scarlet, they shall be as white as snow." Isaiah 1:18.

All have sinned. No one is righteous (Romans 3:10) "For God has consigned all men to disobedience that He may have mercy on us all." Romans 11:32.

"While we were yet helpless, at the right time Christ died for the ungodly. God shows His *love* for us in that *while we were yet sinners* Christ died for us." Romans 5:8

While we were *yet sinners*! Truly, this is amazing grace!

Jesus didn't *have* to die. But he *did* have to die in order to redeem us. So He chose to die.

"What wondrous love is this, oh my soul!"

*

Rest

"There remains a rest for the people of God." Hebrews 4:4.

God wants you to have a soul at rest.

Your past, present and future are safe in Jesus Christ.

You can give a huge sigh of relief.

Now He wants you to learn to trust in Him, day by day. Trust is the bedrock of Sabbath rest. Trust is the way to peace.

"Thou wilt keep him in perfect peace whose mind is stayed on Thee because he *trusts* in Thee."

Isaiah 26:3

"What time I am afraid, I put my trust in Thee."

Psalm 56:3

"Trust in the Lord with all your heart." Proverbs 3:5 "I have trusted in thy steadfast love; my heart shall rejoice in thy salvation." Psalms 13: 5

*

Ana

When our daughter, Ana, was about three or four years old, her Dad and I frequently told her, "We love you." Maybe we said it *too* often, because at bedtime one night when I said "I love you, sweetie," she answered with exaggerated patience: "I *know* you love me. But are you *happy* at me?"

I told my friend Jane about this and she said, "That's it exactly. I know God *loves* me, because He is God and He *is* love. He loves everyone. But I wish I could know if He is happy at me?"

Get ready for some gospel good news. You are God's child, and He *is* happy with you. He delights in you. He rejoices over you with singing! Zephaniah 3:17.

Are you perfect? Of course not. He is still happy with you, you are still His own child; His love never ends. You are a joy to Him.

I hope you will read Psalm 139. God formed you in your mother's womb. Listen to the intimacy:

"My frame was not hidden from Thee when I was being made in secret, intricately wrought in the depths of the earth. Thy eyes beheld my unformed substance; in Thy book were written, every one of them, the days that were formed for me, when as yet there was none of them. How precious to me are Thy thoughts, O God! When I awake, I am still with Thee."

"I have loved you with an everlasting love," God explains. "Therefore I have continued my faithfulness to you." Jeremiah 31:3.

His love for you is everlasting. Nothing can deter it, nothing can hinder it. Not even you.

St. Paul wrote, "Who shall separate us from the love of Christ? I am fully persuaded that neither death nor life, nor angels, nor principalities...

nor *anything else* in all creation, will be able to separate us from the love of God in Christ Jesus our Lord." Romans 8:35-39.

Begin to believe this and watch what happens inside your soul. You may run into doubts. Remember, ask God to help you if you feel unbelief.

"By this we shall know that we are of the truth, and reassure our hearts before Him whenever our hearts condemn us, for God is greater than our hearts, and He knows all things." 1 John 3:19.

Let Him work this precious knowledge into your heart, like a potter molding clay. Relax in His hands and let Him shape you.

*

Being Still

I had the pleasure of taking pottery classes both in college and in the Community Arts Center. It was a wonderful(and frustrating) experience.

The hardest part, for me, was centering the clay. It has to be perfectly centered under your hands. Then you can make any number of amazing things from simple clay!

God wants to center us in His hands. When the clay is centered it becomes quiet, even though it is moving very fast. It doesn't resist the potter's hands. It yields.

"Be still and know that I am God." Psalm 46:10.

Going back to my friend Jane's question. Is God happy with you? Yes. Does God approve everything you do and say? No. But He remembers our frame, He knows that we are dust. We are clay. He forgives. He is still *happy* that you are His child. He loves you with an everlasting love. Nothing in Heaven or earth can change that. Ever. Not even you. *That's* the beautiful truth.

*

Security

There is perfect security in belonging to Jesus. Nothing will make Him change his mind about wanting you and loving you. And He watches over you, in His own words, "like a hen gathers her chicks under her wing." Matthew 23:37.

Jesus didn't *have* to die on the cross. He was willing to. Why? Because that was the only way to redeem all the world. It was His holy work to do, the reason He came into this world. He said, "No one takes my life from me; I lay it down of my own accord." John 10:18.

This was the plan from the beginning of creation. The Holy Lord, three in one, knew that mankind would fall and fail in the garden of Eden. I wonder if there was some discussion about this, about whether to give man freedom of choice at all. But the final decision was yes, to create man and later to redeem him. Why? Because redemption in Jesus is far more beautiful than mere perfection.

*

The Cross

I have heard people say that Father God turned away His face from Jesus on the cross, because God is holy and cannot look on sin. I do not believe that. For many reasons. Father God would *never* forsake Jesus. And there is nothing He cannot do. The Bible says God looks over the world, beholding the good *and* the evil. Proverbs 15:3.

So why did Jesus cry out, "My God, My God, why hast Thou forsaken me?" Psalms 22:1.

As he often did, he was quoting scripture to show that this was fulfillment of prophecy. Psalm 22 goes on to say "Yet, Thou art holy. Enthroned on the praises of Israel." Psalms 22:3.

Psalm 22 continues with more right on target prophecy about the passion and death of Jesus: that none of his bones should be broken; that he was mocked and despised and taunted with these words:"He committed his cause to the Lord; let Him deliver him; let Him rescue him, for He delights in Him!" Psalm 22:8.

It goes on to say "They have pierced my hands and feet" (verse 16) "they divide my garments among them, and for my raiment they cast lots."

Now look at verse 24 of this same psalm: "For He [God] has *not* despised or abhorred the affliction of the afflicted; and He has not *hid* His face from him, but has heard, when He cried to Him."

At the Last Supper, Jesus told his disciples they would all forsake Him."Yet I am not alone, for the Father is with me." John 16:32.

The Father would never abandon the Son. Neither will He abandon you, His redeemed child.

"For the Lord has comforted His people and will have compassion on His afflicted." Isaiah 49:13.

"Fear not, for I have redeemed you. I have called you by name, you are Mine. When you pass through the waters I will be with you; and through the rivers, they shall not overwhelm you…. for I am the Lord your God…. you are precious in My eyes, and honored, and I love you." Isaiah 43:1-4. RSV.

It's the beautiful truth.

*

A Small Miracle

There is certainly no given formula for how to pray. Christ gave us the best one in the Lord's Prayer. But when we are face to face with a crisis, we mostly just cry from our hearts. "Likewise the Spirit helps us; for we do not know how to pray as we ought, but the Sprit himself intercedes for us with sighs too deep for words." Romans 8:26,27.

One of the tenderest experiences I ever had with prayer was when our cocker spaniel presented us with a litter of mixed puppies. One of them became sickly and quickly worsened. I had named him Timothy and I brought him into the kitchen and laid him on a blanket covered with newspaper. I stroked him lightly and prayed desperately for God to heal him. He was by now no longer conscious. This was many years ago, before all-night emergency vets.

I prayed and I begged. Nothing helped. Then something in my heart "gave." I stopped begging for the puppy to get well. I no longer felt grieved or frightened. I committed Timothy to God, and just asked that He comfort the little fellow. I continued to stroke him, simply pouring my love into him, no longer asking for anything.

Abruptly, he began to leak bloody urine. I was sure the end had come. Then, to my amazement, he opened his eyes and stumbled to his feet. The stained urine poured, and he began to walk around! Soon he was indicating he wanted food!

Timothy recovered completely. I felt God teaching me something through this experience—something without words. Something about love being the great healing power, and perfect love casting out fear. 1John 4:18

*

Angels

People wonder about angels. The Bible assures us that they are real and they serve God perfectly. As glorious as they are, *we* are even more special to God than the angels. We are His own children.

I had an experience once that shocked me. I was praying for the hurting children all over the world. The Holy Spirit really does help us to pray.

Guided by the Holy Spirit, I made an unusual request of God—I asked that He would send His angels to all the suffering children to meet their varying needs and to comfort them.

I didn't even finish the sentence before I had a sensation of a rush of angels coming from heaven to earth. They were countless—maybe millions, maybe more. It was as if they had been poised at heaven's gate waiting for someone's prayer to propel them into action. They had been longing to get this commission. I was staggered. I had known that God loves for us to participate in His work and in His love, but I never thought our prayers could be so far-reaching. I made a mental note to pray much more often. To try to pray without ceasing, as the Bible urges us to do. 1Thessalonians 5:17

*

In God's Time

One of my most amazing experiences also involved angels. That is the only explanation I can come up with for the incredible thing that happened.

I had met a very lonely lady at a Christian Yoga Camp. Her name was Jacqueline. She was oppressed with sadness. We talked a lot. The cloud never lifted even a little. When the weekend camp ended, we exchanged addresses; but a significant period of time passed with no communication between us.

I remember I was pregnant with Ana when I lay down one afternoon to rest. Immediately I heard the Lord's voice in my spirit, instructing me to write to Jacqueline and assure her that Jesus loved her dearly. The impression was so strong, I could not rest until I had written the note and sealed the envelope. I found her address, and the only thing lacking was a stamp. We were out completely. I left the letter on the shelf dividing the entry and the dining room and lay back down to rest.

I didn't remember the letter until a couple of days later. Then I couldn't find it. I berated myself for having delayed; I asked my husband if he had mailed it. No, he had not even seen it.

Maybe the whole experience was all my imagination, I reasoned—not a real message from God. Maybe I had dozed and dreamed it. So it didn't matter really.

I put it out of my mind.

Three months passed. Then a letter came in the mail from Jacqueline— the first ever. She wrote that she had just received my note dated three months ago. It arrived somehow in her mail box, she explained—without a stamp and without a postmark!

But, she wrote, she received it at the exact time when she needed it most, and it was a tremendous comfort and reassurance to her.

As I recall, I just covered my face with my hands. I could not even think of words to pray at that moment—but my heart was saying Thank You.

*

Banjo

One of my favorite angel stories is a funny one. Can an animal be an angel? Well, not exactly, but God can use them in a similar capacity. He used Balaam's donkey, enabling him to speak. And in my life he used a big, gangly dog named Banjo.

Our first house was near a large lake, where I loved to walk. At the end of the walk I made a loop back around to our house. This was one area where there were no houses or cross-streets—just a paved road through massive trees and a thicket of shrubbery and undergrowth. It was beautiful, but isolated.

There was a huge dog in our neighborhood which was part Great Dane, I believe, and part St. Bernard, and who knows what else. He was enormous. And he loved better than life to go walking with me.

Now, I love animals. But the problem was he slurped my hand and bumped against me on every walk, nearly knocking me over again and again.

I tried to sneak out of the house unnoticed. No way. Banjo had a radar for when I wanted to go for a walk. He was at my side in an instant.

One evening, a little later than usual, Banjo and I went walking partway around the lake and then back home and around the loop. I noticed it was getting dusky and I felt a little uneasy, which was not like me.

Sure enough, a man in a red convertible pulled up beside me and slowed down. My heart pounded with anxiety, but I just looked ahead and kept walking.

"Want a ride?" he asked.

"No, thank you, I'm walking for exercise."

I did not look at him. I thought, this is the telling point. If his intentions are honest, he will drive on.

But he stayed beside me, still driving at about 3 mph. "I'll be glad to give you a ride."

"Thank you, no."

But the stranger *still* did not drive on.

The next thing he said took me by surprise:"Is that your dog?"

Immediately I put my hand on Banjo's head and confidently lied:"Yes, he is."

That was all it took. The man in the car sped up and was gone from sight.

How I loved that dog from that day on! I hugged him and he slobbered and drooled on me and together we hurried for home. And I cut the woodsy loop out of my daily walk.

*

Homesick

A round mid-life I ran into trouble. I developed Chronic Fatigue Syndrome, with its low-grade fever, aches and pains, sore throat, and debilitating fatigue. I began having to cancel choir practice(I was the choir director and keyboard artist at our small church). Finally I had to take a leave of absence. I could not even attend church, much less plan and perform the music.

There were other factors, too. A beloved, close uncle died. Then my best friend died. I was eventually overwhelmed by serious depression. I was even hospitalized for it. I no longer wanted to live. I did not feel close to God on this earth, and I longed for Heaven. I was home-sick.

What a heavy burden my illness must have been on my dear family! But I couldn't shake it off.

St. Paul talks about being homesick for Heaven. But then he chooses life here on earth, as being more helpful to the people here. So it is not a sin to look forward to our Heavenly Home. Not at all!

But it *is* a sin to crave release from this world to the point that we turn away from engaging in life.

One night at the hospital I had a beautiful vision of pure golden light. I was given to understand that this was God's mercy. I was being allowed to see it visually, as far as such a thing was possible. I was mesmerized by the beauty and purity of the vision. It was like gold, like jewelry, but also transparent like light.

Then I heard a voice in my spirit:"The pure, sweet mercy of God is falling like a sweet spring rain over this entire poor, broken planet."

I knew the voice was truth. And I knew I was going to be asked at some point to tell others about it. That meant I was not at my home-coming time yet. I was disappointed.

I scribbled the words on a scrap of paper and addressed it to my dear friend and prayer partner, Lee. I would get my mom to mail it. Maybe Lee could deliver the message to the world and I could still go Home. But I had a sneaky suspicion it would not turn out that way.

Sure enough, I lived. Still longing for Heaven.

When I told my young friend Eva about the vision, she said, "It's like the song!" Eva attended a different church from ours. I had never heard the little chorus she then sang for me. The words were uncannily similar. Yet I had never heard the song.

*

Repentance

I spent a week in the hospital and very nearly died from accidental overdose of different medications they tried on me. However, I survived, and came home, and God helped me heal.

Not long afterward—a few weeks maybe—my same young friend Eva took me to a Father's Love Conference. It was life-changing! She took me back again that night to hear more.

The leader, Jack, taught that if you have ever felt "home-sick" for heaven, or wished you could just die and be finished with this world, that this was actually a death- wish, and it could even be sin.

Sin! I knew I had sins, but I didn't know this was one of them. I went to the altar at prayer time.

Jack led all of us who qualified in a group prayer. I found myself *repenting* with tears.

I was heartbroken to think I had wanted something so different from what my Father in Heaven wanted for me. I begged His forgiveness—and *received* it. *Receiving* is so absolutely essential for healing to come. Honestly, I don't know how I *received* it. It seems like God did the receiving part for me, as well as the giving. I just know that the anguish left me and joy came in its place. Yes, real joy!

That very night the entire heaviness lifted off of me. The wrong desire left me completely. God forgave and healed me that night.

I have loved life ever since. I've been through some hard times, but that desire to escape has not returned. Instead, when times are hard, I run to my Father God and He helps me cope until the joy returns.

Jack is in Heaven now. When I see him again I will tell him how God used his teaching and prayer to completely change my life and set me free. God can do that for you, too, be assured. Let it be a *blessed assurance*!

*

"Today I set before you life and death; therefore choose life." Deuteronomy 30:19.

Life is what God wants for you. When your time here is fulfilled *He* will bring you home. He already knows all the days of your life and the exact number of them; He has had them written in His book since long before you were born. Psalm 139. That is another blessed assurance.

*

Crisis Of Faith

Now my narrative reverts way back to my college days. When I was a sophomore in college I had a severe crisis of faith.

I was attending First Presbyterian on an Easter Sunday, and there was much celebration about how terribly Jesus suffered and died so *we* could go free. In my theological immaturity, I took offense at this, not understanding that Jesus was not forced to lay down His life, but gave it most *willingly* to save us.

I left the church for *four years*.

I studied B'hai, Taoism, Buddhism and other paths during that time. I got way off track. But through it all, I loved Jesus. And He loved me.

Mistakenly, my tender feelings for Jesus were the reason I turned my back on God. Boy, did I have a lot to learn!

One afternoon, walking past the same Presbyterian church, I had an impulse to see if the chapel door was unlocked. It was! At no other time have I found it so. I loved the grey stone chapel with its stained glass windows, so I went in. It was empty. Self-consciously, I walked up to the big Bible on the pulpit. Colored light from the window behind it streamed over the pages. I didn't touch the Bible, because I reasoned someone may have left it open to the lesson they planned to deliver that night. But my eye fell on a key passage. I wish I could remember what it said. I don't. But I knew through it that Father God was drawing me to come back to Him.

That very Wednesday night I walked to the church (I didn't have a car in college) for the small chapel service. I sat on the back row. After a lesson and scripture, they asked for suggestions for hymns to sing. I knew right away I longed to hear#303—Be Thou My Vision, my favorite since childhood. But I was much too shy to speak up.

God understood. An older person closer to the front raised his hand and requested—you guessed it, of course—#303. My heart pounded, knowing that this was no coincidence. Gratefully, I sang these words:

> Be Thou my vision, O Lord of my heart!
> Nought be all else to me, save that Thou art.
> Thou my best thought by day or by night;
> Waking or sleeping, Thy presence my light.
> Be Thou my wisdom, and Thou my true word.
> I ever with Thee and Thou in me, Lord.
> Thou my great Father, I Thy true son,
> Thou in me dwelling and I with thee One.
> High King of Heaven, my victory won;
> may I reach Heaven's joys, O Bright Heaven's sun!
> Heart of my own heart, whatever befall,
> Still be my vision, O Ruler of all.

> —-Ancient Celtic tune; words by E. Hull

Heart of my own heart.

Father God called to me that night and I was forgiven and restored to true Christianity. I didn't have answers to any of my questions yet—but I knew I wanted God to be Heart of my own heart forever.

*

Discovery

Later I learned some wonderful things. I found them in the Bible. First of all, Jesus was with God from the very beginning. "In the beginning was the Word(Jesus). And the Word was with God and the Word *was* God. He was in the beginning with God; through Him all things were made, and without Him was not anything made that was made. In Him was life, and the life was the light of man. The light shines in the darkness and the darkness has not overcome it." John 1:1-5.

Without Him was not anything made! Jesus was in on every detail of the Creation process.

I came to realize that God and Jesus were inseparable.

"I and the Father are One. He who has seen me has seen the Father." John 10:30. He was with the Father long before the foundation of the world. They planned creation together, along with the Holy Spirit, and they were in perfect accord.

In deciding to give man free will, they knew of course that mankind would fall. I can't presume to have any hint of that conversation. But I do know that from the beginning, it was planned that Jesus would give His life to save all the world. He knew what He was volunteering for. It was worth it to Him. He said, later, to His apostles, "For this cause came I into the world." And, "No man takes my life from me; I lay it down of my own accord, and I will take it up again." John 10:18.

I was still troubled for a little while about the cross.

But Jesus was my heart and is my heart. And I have come to understand that everything we saw in Jesus is also true of the Father. So I believed Jesus. And my distrust of God began to heal. I understood that it was not so much God sending His son down to die on the cross—but it was God Himself who came down and died on that cross. For they are one.

It cost him dearly. In the Garden of Gethsemane, Jesus begged His Father God that if salvation could be accomplished by some other means, please to deliver Him from the horror of crucifixion. You know the famous line of His surrender, His obedience:"Nevertheless, not my will but Thine be done." Luke 22:42.

I believe if He had to do it all over again, He would. I believe if He had to do it to save just one lost soul—just you, just me—He would. So great is His love!

The Bible promises that Jesus will "…look on the fruit of the travail of His soul and be satisfied."

When He sees us, redeemed, He is like a happy mother of a newborn child. He has no regrets about the cross.

And me? I am so thankful to Him for what He did for all of us! I love Him more than ever.

*

Belonging

I am sure it took many years for me to come to a place of real trust in God the Father. I don't mean perfect trust—I wish I did. I'm still working on that.

Sometimes I hear people ask, "God knows everything; why did He create the world and people in the first place, when He already knew we would sin?"

I love this question, because I love the answer.

When God created Eden, it was perfection. Yes, we wish we had kept it that way. But we didn't. And God allowed the fall because He knew of something more beautiful and more wonderful than mere perfection. Redemption.

*

"*While we were yet sinners*, Christ loved us and gave Himself for us." Wow. And now that we are redeemed, we belong to Him.

"For Christ Jesus has made me His own." Phil. 3:12. To *belong* to Jesus, bought by His blood, amazes me and fills me with joyful wonder!

*

One Thing I Know

When I better realized how much Jesus loves God His Father, and how much the two are one, I began to get over being mad at God. I even began to slowly trust Him.

I realized this one day when I was reading John 9:25. Suddenly the words seemed to jump off the page. They were like living things! The high priests were asking the blind man(whom Jesus had just healed)"don't you know this man is a sinner?"

The man responded: "Whether He is a sinner I do not know. One thing I know. I was blind before and now I see."

One thing I know. God seemed to be asking me to build my personal theology starting with one certainty. Surprisingly, I did know one thing. I knew that *God is Good.* I knew it absolutely and to the depths of my being. I knew it because *Jesus* is good. And now I had something to stand on, something very solid: God is good, all good, all the time. "There is no shadow or variation of change in Him." James 1:17. "Even if we are faithless, He remains faithful." 2 Timothy 2:13." "God is light, in Him is no darkness at all."1 John 1:5.

An older lady in my prayer group used to say, "God is altogether trustworthy."

I had come a long way. But I had a long way to go, and undoubtedly still do.

*

Trust

Learning to trust God is the ultimate lesson in being a true Christian. It makes all the difference.

All through the Bible, Old testament and New, God urges us to trust Him. Jesus asks the same thing, often substituting the word "believe." "Said I not unto you, *only believe* and ye shall see the glory of God?" He said in the moments before He raised Lazarus from the dead.

How are we to trust Him? We know that bad things happen to both Christians and non-Christians. Accidents occur. Troubles come. Jesus even told us to expect them.

"In the world ye will have tribulation, but be of good cheer—I have overcome the world!" John 16:33.

He also said, "Let not your heart be troubled, neither let it be afraid. Ye believe in God, believe also in Me." John 14:1

The key to trusting God in the bad times lies in Romans 8:28. "We know that in everything God works for good with those who love Him."

Going way back to Genesis, Joseph essentially told his brothers, "You meant it for evil, but God meant it for good." And, "Rest assured, do not be afraid." Genesis 43:23.

When evil comes into our lives, God re-shapes it, re- works it, redeems it—until it becomes something worthy of our praise.

"For everything he does is worthy of our praise."

This illustration has been used before, and it is a good one: we see, as it were, only the wrong side of a great tapestry being woven. Tangled masses of threads, clashing colors, knots—a disastrous mess. But when the master weaver displays the front side of his laborious work, it is perfectly, breathtakingly beautiful, every thread in place.

We have to understand that we are not yet capable of seeing the big picture. But God is. He is the great Savior-Redeemer. It is my personal belief that if He cannot ultimately bring a greater good out of trials that come into the lives of His children, He will not allow those trials to occur.

*

Mercy

One of my favorite Bible stories takes place in the Garden of Gethsemane. Only Luke records the full drama.

Luke 22:10. Peter, with his usual reckless devotion, sliced off the ear of the high priest's slave.

But Jesus said, "No more of this!" And He touched the man's ear and *healed* him! With His whole life crumbling around him, Jesus took time to heal the ear of an enemy! What kindness and caring! What pure and perfect love! God allowed Peter to sever the ear because He knew His Son would heal it. I am certain that this soldier's life was changed forever. Surely he became a believer.

*

Dreams

Ilost my dad when I was three years old. Later, in adulthood, I had a dream that I was a barefoot, ragged little girl in a dirty white shift, waiting in a train station. I clearly believed my dad would come on the next train. But trains came and went, and no one came for me.

I was looking down at the floor, becoming hopeless, when a man in a white linen robe approached me from the right.

It was Jesus. He knelt on one knee and talked to me quietly. He explained that I was to come with Him, now, and He would take good care of me.

Reluctantly I put my cold hand in His big, warm one, and walked at His side. But with the honesty of a three-year- old, I told Him that I would rather have my own Daddy. He said simply, "I know."

When I woke up I was astonished at the dream. At how Jesus "adopted me," making me His own. He will do that for you, too, you only have to ask. But more than anything I was amazed at His humility. Jesus—King of Kings—willing to be second best!

"What wondrous love is this, O my soul!"

I believe that Jesus was extending that unconditional love and acceptance to the child in me. He does not want to be second best to anything or anyone once we have become mature Christians. Because He knows only His own love can satisfy the deep longings of our hearts. But He understands very tenderly the workings of a child's heart.

*

Near-Death Moments

Jesus did take me "under His wing." Even before that dream. When I was two-years-old and my family was still complete, I came down with pneumonia. I had a fever of 105. While my mother and father drove me to the hospital, I lay on the back seat singing"Jesus loves me, this I know…"

My mother tells me now that she was terrified by this, fearing it meant that I was dying.

It turned out that I was near to death. The doctor told my parents that if they had delayed any longer in getting me to the hospital, they would have lost me that night. But they were praying for me. They were believers.

I had another near-death experience even before that.

My mother's ob-gyn was on vacation when she went into labor with me. A young, much less experienced doctor replaced him. I first heard this story when I was an adult. I learned that when I was born, I didn't breathe. The young doctor gave me mouth to mouth resuscitation for *five minutes*! And finally I drew a breath.

When I heard this story, God spoke to me in my spirit.

He spoke not with words, but with a sure knowing.

The older, very experienced doctor would have given up on me. He had lost babies before. It was the nature of things that not every baby lived.

But the young, untried doctor refused to give up. He refused to lose this baby. He kept on, persistently, until at last he did get me to breathe on my own!

I mention these two stories because heaven feels so comfortable and familiar to me. I think I have dim memories of having been there. I will share those with you more later on.

*

Where This World Ends

"I will pour out my Spirit on all flesh: your sons and your daughters shall prophecy, your old men shall dream dreams, and your young men shall see visions. Even upon the menservants and the maidservants in those days; I will pour out my Spirit." Joel 2:28-29.

I have very vivid dreams, always have had. One was a recurring dream, beginning when I was about six years old.

In it, I was walking down a path in a thick forest. The ground was irregular and a little steep. It bent to the left as I walked downhill. Suddenly on the right side of the forest path I saw an old abandoned wheelbarrow, with gardening instruments placed inside, not to be used anymore. I understood it was a sign or symbol of rest. Cessation of works. Sabbath. "So, then, there remains a Sabbath rest for the people of God; for whoever enters God's rest also ceases from his labors as God did from His." Hebrews 4:9,10.

To my left, the path bent into a clear glen full of sunlight and soft, low-cut grass. I never was able to make that turn or see fully what was there. But I knew Jesus was standing there, waiting for me; and the path ended there in a circle of light. I longed to reach the place where He was. In my dream it was understood to be "the place where this world ends." It was all very mysterious. And I had this same dream at various times in my life.

As best I can understand, the meaning was that I should put aside my works and my striving for my own sanctification, and simply rest my soul in the Presence of Christ, and *His* completed work.

Looking around me I saw many good Christians striving like I had been, unable to rest, unable to trust that Jesus could love them while they were resting in Him; that He could really love us apart from our works for Him.

"Therefore, while the promise of *entering His rest remains*, let us fear lest any of you be judged to have failed to reach it. For the good news came to us just as to them; but the message which they heard did not benefit them, because it did not meet with faith in the hearers. For we who have *believed* enter that *rest*." Hebrews 4:1-3.

How healing it is to let God be God.

When we rest in God, it is an expression of faith. We don't try to achieve righteousness on our own merits. We know we don't have to. We know that we can't!

When we rest in the Lord, the works that we do for Him will be an outpouring of thanksgiving, of reciprocated love. There will be joy in serving Him, because our offerings are no longer driven by guilt or fear. Our hearts will be at rest in His mercy and grace.

*

Hearts-Ease

There is a little purple-yellow-white flower which is known as viola. It's like a miniature pansy, or a multi-colored violet. Some call it johnny-jump-up.

There is another, more old-fashioned name for this humble flower— one which is rarely heard: hearts-ease.

Hearts-ease. That sounds so beautiful to me.

My friend Lee and I began to use this term in our prayers. Doesn't it describe what we long for? And yearn for our loved ones to have?

Hearts-ease is a gift from Heaven. We find it more and more as we learn to trust in Jesus.

What do we need to trust? That He is all good, all the time. That He is altogether God, and can do anything.

That whatever happens in our lives, He will turn it into good because we love Him and He loves us. That He loves us with an everlasting love, from which nothing can separate us. And finally, that the passion and death of Jesus Christ was *fully sufficient* to cover all sin, past, present or future, and to "present us faultless before the Presence of His glory, with exceeding joy." Jude: vs.24

Jesus has already done everything necessary. Our part is to believe with thankful hearts, and to rejoice. And share the *beautiful truth* in every way we can.

St. Francis of Assisi said, "Preach the gospel at all times; if necessary, use words." Sometimes a kind word or just a smile is the best presentation of the gospel for a given moment in time.

There is even a verse for times when we fall prey to old feelings of guilt or shame over things God has already forgiven: 1John 3:19-20

"By this we shall know that we are of the truth, and reassure our hearts before Him whenever our hearts condemn us, for God is greater than our hearts and He knows everything."

Hearts-ease.

I wish it for you today.

Hearts-ease is what I would have found in my recurring dream in which a walk in the forest ended in a glen of light. I knew Jesus was around that corner. But I never reached that far in the dream.

Maybe I never parked my "wheelbarrow" and left my tools inside. The striving to accomplish something can haunt us in both daylight hours and night dreams.

My husband has had to remind me to put the tools in the wheelbarrow and get some rest while I've been working on this manuscript!

One birthday I asked my daughter Ana to give me an assortment of greeting cards that I could send. She was working at a Christian book store and received a discount. All the cards she chose were beautiful. One was very outstanding.

To start with, it was round in shape. On the front was a painting of two robins feeding their young in a nest in a corner of a potting shed.

But the surprise came when I opened the card.

I was startled to see a picture of a wheelbarrow completely surrounded by light, the tools placed inside! I had never told Ana about my dream.

The verse read: "Cast your cares on the Lord and He will sustain you." Psalm 55:22.

That card I never sent. That card I kept.

*

Believing

Believe. How often did Jesus urge His disciples and followers to believe? Sometimes it was expressed as "Only believe," as if it were either something very simple, or something utterly essential. Probably both.

Oh, to have been there! To hear Him say those words.

He says them still.

"Let not your heart be troubled. Ye believe in God, believe also in Me." John 14:1.

Jesus wants us to trust Him in every circumstance. With an innocent, child-like trust. Children were naturally drawn to Jesus, and He loved them and blessed them. We long for His love and blessing, but do we believe we have them?

"Only believe."

*

Be Still

I f you don't have the *beautiful truth*, then what is the "truth" you have? Maybe it is something you picked up in Sunday School and church that causes you anxiety and stress. Do you tend to feel guilty and unworthy?

Some of us were trained that way in church, sad to say. Do you feel that nothing you do is sufficient to please God? Another flawed teaching.

"Be still and know that I am God." Psalm 46:10.

It is all right to be still and contemplate the perfect love of God which surrounds and indwells you. You are loved—tenderly. Stop striving so hard for awhile and just consider what a blessing it is to be His beloved child. To have a Father you can trust, that you can talk to, and Who hears you attentively.

God is so good. You can talk to Him about anything; He hears and He cares. And He helps. No prayer is unanswered. There is yes, no, and sometimes wait. But whatever His answer, it is for your perfect good and eternal happiness.

Remember, Jesus cautioned us, "In this world you will have tribulation; but be of good cheer, for I have overcome the world!" John 16:30.

He doesn't want us to be surprised or discouraged when hard times come. They come to every person. It is not a sign that you have done wrong—or right. It's the way of this world, ever since the Fall. But God is weaving everything together into pure *goodness*. And He has prepared a wonderful place for us to live for eternity where there will be no more sorrow or pain or separation.

No more tears and no more fears.

*

Heaven

If I have visited Heaven, it was when I was an infant or a very young child, when I came close to death several times. I have read and readily believe the stories of people who have had beautiful afterlife experiences. I don't have anything that precise. No hard, fast memories. But I have impressions; and such a great love for our eternal home that, for awhile, it was a little scary. I actually thought I wanted to be there instead of here. God has healed that, without dimming my love for Heaven.

What is Heaven like? People have so many questions. But the first one is generally this:

Will we know each other?

Absolutely yes. We will have bodies, not of clay, but real bodies—of a Heavenly substance. Remember that after his Resurrection, Jesus walked through a locked door, and He also ate fish. This type of body is impossible for us to really understand. But He demonstrated it, so it wouldn't be just a theory or a hope. We will talk, sing, dance, do work that we love, and laugh. A lot. Because of something funny? Probably sometimes, but mostly we will laugh for pure joy.

In visions and dreams I've had of Heaven I have heard children playing on a grassy green hill. Their games were not competitive. There was no arguing or contesting; there was happy laughter. The games were along the lines of sailing wooden boats down a stream, flying kites, or tossing a ball. It was delightful to hear their musical laughter!

*

More Dreams

Heaven and dreams are closely entwined in my mind. I had a dream of my grandmother when she was very ill. I was carrying her down a wooded hill to a train station; she was lying across both my arms like a large child. When we got to the station, I saw lots of my family gathered around to see her off. People had cameras and were taking photographs. And I saw my grandfather seated on the train. He had died about 20 years earlier. I tried to get on the train with my grandmother. I had every intention of going with her, I loved her so dearly! But she said to me, "No, it is time for me to go with *him* now."

She took a seat beside her husband, and I had to step off the train.

*

At the end of her life here, my grandmother weighed only seventy-two pounds, and she could not bear her own weight to stand up or walk. She had to be carried from the bed to the chair and fed through a tube. My uncle drove me from South Carolina to Virginia. Grandmother was living at home, still, and my patient mother was responsible for all her care. I wanted to help. And I wanted to be with them both.

As weak as she was, and in pain, my grandmother smiled when she saw me. My mom prompted "Isn't it nice to have Lynn here?" and my grandmother closed her eyes and whispered: "Like an angel from heaven." You can understand why I loved her so.

It was a great blessing to be with her those last four days. It was during Eastertide. When I saw that she couldn't stand up, I knew God had prepared me for this time with great kindness through the dream where

I was carrying her to the train. I knew her time was very near. She passed into Heaven on Maundy Thursday of Holy Week, in my arms. It was sad, but also sweet, to see her finally at rest. She had suffered very much.

But no more pain for her, no more sorrow; the joy of being rejoined with loved ones. And the wondrously beautiful welcoming face of Jesus.

*

Other Dreams

S ome time later I had another dream about my grandmother.
In this one, she was in Heaven, strong and healthy, living in a kind of very nicely furnished apartment(for lack of a better word). Light streamed out the door and windows. It seemed to be built into the side of a green hill.

She greeted me wearing a green and gold embroidered house coat, with her silver-white hair piled gracefully on her head. She was much younger than the age when she passed. She seemed to be approximately in the prime of life.

I woke and knew this was no ordinary dream. I knew I had visited my grandmother in heaven.

When my father-in-law died, it was very sudden. We were all stunned. He had a heart attack early on a Sunday morning. An ambulance was summoned, but he was deceased upon arrival at the hospital.

The afternoon of his funeral I took a short nap. To my surprise, he came to me in a dream. It was face to face, as if he were close-up on a television screen. He was wearing a huge smile, just like he used to in this life.

He spoke to me. His voice was his own distinct voice, complete with a colloquialism in his tone and vocabulary that was unique to him.

"Give your mind some ease," he encouraged me. "Everything is all right!"

That was all. I woke. But there was something about his "everything is all right" that seemed to include all of creation—everything. As if he had seen the completed side of the tapestry, and knew that it all turns out beautiful and perfect. I was deeply consoled by the clear, almost child-like delight in his face. He had seen for himself the *beautiful truth*.

*

When my mother-in-law passed, she was in a nursing home. My husband, Ron, had gone to take care of some business matters and I was alone with Grace. She was unconscious and her breathing was shallow and soundless.

"Talk to her," the hospice nurse encouraged me. "The hearing is the last thing to go."

With no one around I felt free to talk to her softly, assuring her of our love for her and God's great love. Then it occurred to me to sing quietly to her. I glanced over my shoulder to be sure that we were still alone.

I had been music minister at a small church for ten years and I had memorized a large repertoire of hymns and worship songs. I sang one after another, for almost two hours; and still no one interrupted us. I began a Maranatha praise song:

"I love you, Lord, and I lift my voice
to worship you, oh my soul rejoice;
take joy, my King, in what you hear;
let it be a sweet, sweet song in your ear."

As I ended this verse she drew a final breath. It was so gentle, soundless, motionless—not even a sigh.

I was holding her hand and I felt a sensation transfer from her to me as she arrived in Heaven. Her joy was boundless! And she was so surprised! A fact which has always delighted me.

Until her latter years she had lacked certainty that she would go to heaven. She had grown up with a scary theology. Then two ministers from our church visited her and talked and prayed with her. She never worried again. She had received the *blessed assurance*.

Even so, she had never dared to dream that Heaven was so wonderful, so happy and delightful!

Through the connection between us, which I can only assume was because I was still holding her hand—she seemed to be trying to get her spiritual balance between the overflow of joy, love and peace which seemed to be equally abundant in Heaven, and almost overwhelming.

I began to cry, suddenly wanting to go with her. I had a lapse into my old homesickness for Heaven.

But I had to get a grip on myself and prepare to tell my husband that his mother had just passed into Heaven.

*

Jane

One night after her death, I dreamed of my friend Jane. She had been sick for so many years. Prior to her illness she was a social butterfly. She loved nothing more than to cook and have people over for dinner.

In my dream, Jane was young again, hosting a party in her Heavenly living room. She was leaning on the sofa, laughing with friends. She wore a red plaid dress with a bright red bow in her hair. Red was her favorite color in this world, too.

When I knew her, Jane had been unable to entertain for decades. Now she was in her element.

*

Jesus

The most wonderful thing about Heaven is Jesus. And I think the most wonderful visible thing about Jesus must be His eyes overflowing with compassion and His beautiful smile full of joy. I have seen these in visions and even attempted to paint a watercolor of His face once. Nothing can reproduce His beauty. I have seen a few paintings(not my own) that I felt definitely resembled Him.

In Isaiah 53:2,3 there is a verse that says "He had no form or comeliness that man should look at Him and no beauty that we should desire Him."

People have interpreted this to mean He was homely. I believe it is referring to His face after the beating and the bleeding from the crown of thorns;

Anyone who saw The Passion of the Christ will understand this revulsion to the battered Christ. The verses in Isaiah go on to say," He was despised and rejected by men; a man of sorrows, and acquainted with grief, and as one from whom men hide their faces. Surely He has borne out griefs and carried our sorrows." The whole chapter is about the Passion of Christ. Isaiah 53.

In fact, He is the most beautiful of all God's creation. How could anything God *made* be as lovely as God's own Son? His physical form is an expression of perfect love.

*

Dreams Continued

I remember another dream I had some years ago. I hope you are one of those people who find dreams interesting. I was walking along a beach when I saw sharks in the water. I ran toward a rock cliff I saw in the near distance. It was very high, but there were handholds and I was able to climb up.

At the top, on the very edge, was a doorway, a threshold. Someone helped me over this final step of my journey.

I found myself in a tiny little cottage that was built on the edge of the rock, but was entirely safe. Someone took care of me, and I knew it was Jesus, though I never saw His face.

There was a table with a book on it in the tiny living room. I picked up the book but was unable to understand the letters and words in it. The Savior helped me lie down on a small cot to rest, and I felt a safety, a sense of Home, as never before.

Later I found these verses in Psalms 62:5-7 which keenly reminded me of my dream:"For God alone my soul waits in silence. He only is my rock and my salvation, my fortress; I shall not be shaken. On God rests my deliverance and my honor; my mighty rock, my refuge is God."

"Hear my cry, O God, listen to my prayer; from the ends of the earth I call to Thee when my heart is faint. Lead Thou me to the rock that is higher than I; for Thou art my refuge, a *strong tower* against the enemy." Psalms 62:1-3.

*

Animals And Heaven

O ne of the questions I hear most frequently is, do animals go to Heaven? Most assuredly yes. Our animals and pets that we love will be with us in Heaven. God loves them, too. He says in 1 Corinthians 13:8 "Love never ends."

All kinds of animals will be there. But they will all be tame and harmless. Isaiah 11:6-7,9 says,

"The wolf shall dwell with the lamb, and the leopard shall lie down with the kid, and the calf and the lion and the fatling together, and a little child shall lead them. The cow and the bear shall feed; their young shall lie down together; and the lion shall eat straw like the ox....they shall not hurt or destroy in all my holy mountain."

In Zechariah 14:20 it states: In that day, there shall be inscribed on the bells of the horses "Holy to the Lord."

Isn't that wonderful?

A tiny little verse tucked away in a book of prophecy that some people may never read. But to those of us who love animals, it is very important.

And I saved the best for last. In Psalms 36:6 "...man and beast Thou savest, O Lord." There, in black and white, is the beautiful truth again.

*

Redeeming Love

Remember that Jesus was together with God the Father and the Holy Spirit when all of creation was formed. He knew the plan all along. He knew mankind would fail Plan A and that God would implement Plan B. Plan A was perfection. Plan B was something far greater—redemption.

"For this cause came I into the world," Jesus told us.

"God showed His love for us....in that while we were yet sinners, Jesus Christ loved us and gave Himself for us." Romans 5:8.

"No man takes my life from me; I lay it down of my own accord. And if I lay it down, I will take it up again." John 10:18

"I have come that you may have life, and life more abundantly." John 10:10.

And the words of His final prayer with the apostles: "...that the world may know that Thou hast sent me and hast loved them even as Thou hast loved me. Father, I desire that they also whom thou hast given me, may be with me where I am, to behold my glory which Thou hast given me in Thy love for me before the foundation of the world." John 17:24

Jesus prayed these words of deepest trust on the night before His death. He knew the hour had come. But He knew also what His passion and death would accomplish; and that in *love*, God had granted Him glory from *before the foundation of the world.*

*

Eden Redeemed A Sonnet

When creatures wild existed in accord,
and gardens lushly grew beneath the sun;
in Man's first day, a gifting from our Lord,
this world was true perfection, all as one.

Yet in the depths of God's creative mind,
there seemed a yearning, unfulfilled desire;
as something stirred in Him of other kind;
of living water, and baptism of fire.

Thus He allowed perfection to be marred,
that Christ might fill the earth with His compassion;
God's son, who came to teach and heal, was scarred
and crucified by mankind's fallen passion.

Through Christ's forgiving love and Resurrection,
the beauty of God's grace surpassed perfection.

*

Redeeming Love A Sonnet

Softly the mist falls, mild and sweet in spring;
the world is hushed in dusky pre-dawn hours
Soft how the birds begin to stir and sing,
and light comes forth to color all the flowers.

Creator, wise and wonderful, again
has made a virgin day, in Eden's hues;
but this new day is holier far than when
the first was made, all dappled with pure dew.

Perfection was His gift to us, but then—
as if perfection somehow begged for more,
Our Savior came to earth, Himself a man,
to walk beside the Galilean shore.

All other wonders: sun and moon and star,
Our Christ's redeeming love exceeds by far.

*

Golgotha was not a mistake. It was an obedient surrender of Jesus as man to God His beloved Father—reversing, as it were, the rebellion of the original man, Adam.

It was not something Christ was forced to do. He was willing, and more than willing, to pay the price of the perfect rescue of creation. So great is the love He has for you. As he loves the whole world, that much he loves you. It is the beautiful truth. But to enter into this rest, you must *believe*.

If we didn't believe the floor was secure beneath our feet, we wouldn't take another step. We trust in many things every day. If we didn't believe we would get a paycheck, we probably would not go in to work. The fact that we must believe the beautiful truth in order to have the joy of it is not a demand; it is simply fact.

Remember:"Lord Jesus, I believe in your tender love for me. *Help thou mine unbelief.*"

His tender love for you. And for me. It almost seems too marvelous to be true. And we should marvel.

Yet it is the simple, beautiful truth.

*

I worked on this manuscript right up to bedtime last night and then had trouble sleeping.

I woke this morning exhausted. Spirit willing, flesh weak. I prayed "I'm so tired, Lord. I don't want to even think about the book just yet."

I felt His gentle response: Are you learning what you are writing? Put your tools in the wheelbarrow for awhile and come to the place where this world ends. Enter into my rest.

So I am gratefully going back to bed for now.

*

An Intercessor

Today I visited the nursing home again. There are all new people living there, except one lady named Hazel. She still knows who I am and smiles to see me.

I have made dozens of new friends there. I am humbled by the patience some of them exhibit in trying living conditions. They are not all patient; but probably all more so than I would be.

When I approached Lucille she was watching TV. I hugged her and we began to talk. She wanted to talk about Jesus.

"I'm just so happy," she enthused, "to have Jesus, and to know He loves me. He so good! Yes, ma'am. He takes care of me...and, you know, He loves *everybody*!" Praise just spilled out of her mouth and I listened intently.

On an impulse I told her that I was trying to write a book about Jesus, and I would appreciate her prayers. I could see that this tiny little lady covered with various wraps and wearing a man's knit cap was worth more than a thousand angels in God's sight. Her heart was completely captivated by her Lord Jesus.

She grew excited about my book. She promised to pray, and she advised, "Just start in and talk about Jesus. Ask the Holy Spirit to help you. He'll give you the words to say."

I am deeply encouraged, knowing she will be praying for me.

You may remember that when I started this book I wrote a prayer to the Father. I said I had no inspiration, no enthusiasm for tackling such a project. I had my ideas, my beliefs, my experiences—but how to present them in a readable way? I asked God to give me enthusiasm, please, if He really wanted me to write this book.

By that very night, I had my first eleven typed pages. Praise be to God.

My heart's prayer is that this book will help you to believe in Jesus' tender love for you. Only believe. You will find hearts- ease. You will find rest. Aren't you desperate for a little rest? Come to the place where"this world ends." Come to Jesus. Come in a new way! Come believing in His tender love for you—embracing the beautiful truth.

*

Jesus says in Matthew11:28, 29: "Come unto Me, all ye who labor and are heavy laden, and I will give you rest. Take my yoke upon you, and learn from me; for I am gentle and lowly in heart, and you will find *rest for your souls.*"

This is the rest we long for. The hearts-ease He offers when we trust in Him, when we believe in His tender love for us. And when we know He is working everything together for good. There is no reason to be downcast or disheartened. He is Lord. And He loves you.

Yes, tenderly.

*

Diamond In The Dark

If you are going through a hard time, you might benefit from reading Lamentations.

Lamentations is probably the most down-hearted book in the Bible. It is filled with grieving words such as these:"My soul is bereft of peace, I have forgotten what happiness is...my soul continually thinks of it and is bowed down within me." 3:17."Behold, O Lord, for I am in distress, my soul is in tumult, my heart is wrung within me...hear how I groan; there is none to comfort me."

Vs. 1:20"For these things I weep; my eyes flow with tears; for a comforter is far from me...my eyes are spent with weeping; my soul is in tumult; my heart is poured out in grief." vs.1:16- 2:11.

Is your soul bowed down? God bless and help you. Suffering is not new. Reading Lamentations can help you know others have shared your pain. We all go through hard times. We all have tears and sorrows in this world.

But in the middle of sad Lamentations(of all places) are found some of the most beautiful and uplifting verses in the entire Bible! I like to think that God used this setting like a jeweler might use black velvet to accentuate a perfect, brightly glistening diamond:

"But this I call to mind, and therefore I have hope: the steadfast love of the Lord never ceases, His(tender) mercies never come to an end; they are new every morning. Great is Thy faithfulness.''The Lord is my portion,' says my soul,'therefore I will hope in Him.'" Lamentations 3:21-14

How beautiful are these verses of faith and trust. If you are bowed down today, please know that His mercies never come to an end. Dare to have hope for a better tomorrow. We suffer many things in this world, but our Lord promises He will never, ever leave us nor forsake us.

Even in times of sorrow, there is rest in knowing He is with us. Sometimes sorrow is the only thing that makes us cease our labors and come to the place where this world ends. Sorrow makes us seek His rest. He has sent us the Comforter for this purpose, to bring hearts-ease when we need it most.

*

The Secret Things

We sometimes strive so hard to understand, and can even find ourselves disturbed and doubting the absolute Goodness of God when we read certain odd things in the Bible, especially in the Old Testament.

There is an obscure verse tucked away in Deuteronomy 29:29 which I embrace with gratitude.

"The secret things belong to the Lord our God; but the things that are revealed belong to us and to our children for ever."

I am thankful that there are secret things which belong only to our Father God. We are not expected or required to understand everything in this life or in the Bible. There is a rest in that which is very healing to me. I hope it will be for you, too.

*

Home

I don't want anyone to be afraid of death. That's why I have dared to share some extremely personal dreams, visions, and history with you—so you will know what waits for you at the place where this world ends. It is glorious! You will find hearts-ease, peace, joy, and you will be saturated in pure love. You will spend time with Jesus. There is all the time you could ever wish for—eternity. There is no end to Heaven. And it is more beautiful and delightful and more interesting than any place on earth. Jesus paid a tremendous price so that you could be there with Him; and He has paid all your debt. When you get to Heaven, you will be Home. Truly home, for the first time and forever more. Thanks be to God!

*

Well, that is my story. At least some of it. I hope so much it will be a blessing to anyone who reads it.

Today, with all my weaknesses and flaws, I can earnestly pray, "Lord Jesus, I believe in your tender love for me."

My heart has fully absorbed the *beautiful truth*.

I pray that your heart will, too.

*

Blessings For You

"Now unto Him who is able to keep you from falling, and to present you faultless before the presence of His glory with exceeding joy; to the only God, our Savior, through Jesus Christ our Lord, be glory and majesty, dominion and power, both now and forever. Amen."

Jude vs.24,25. kjv

*

"The Lord bless you and keep you; the Lord make His face to shine upon you, and be gracious to you; The Lord lift up his countenance upon you, and give you peace."
Amen.

Numbers 6:24rsv

The End

www.ingramcontent.com/pod-product-compliance
Lightning Source LLC
Chambersburg PA
CBHW031229120626
46545CB00003B/1055